The Easy Book of
FRACTIONS

The Easy Book of
FRACTIONS

by David C. Whitney

illustrated by Sheila Granda

FRANKLIN WATTS, INC.   845 Third Avenue   New York, N.Y. 10022

SBN 531-01842-3

The Easy Book of
FRACTIONS

Everyone uses
FRACTIONS

Musicians use fractions to play music. They have to be able to read half-notes, quarter-notes, eighth-notes, and many others.

Storekeepers use fractions to figure prices, weights, and sizes.

Mothers use fractions when they make things with recipes that call for $\frac{1}{4}$ teaspoon of salt, $\frac{2}{3}$ cup of milk, or $\frac{1}{8}$ pound of butter.

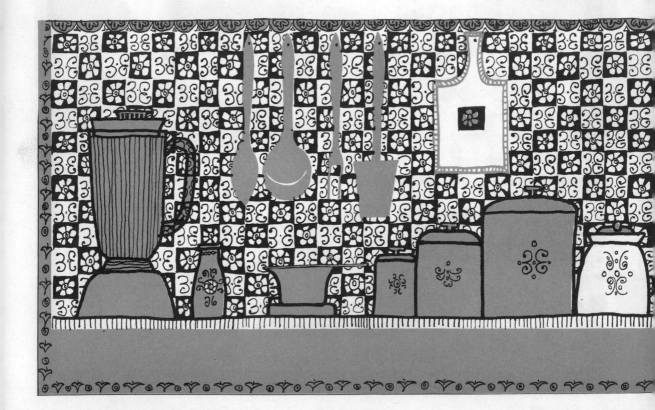

And you use fractions any time you ask your mother or father for a quarter or a half dollar.

A FRACTION

IS PART OF SOMETHING.

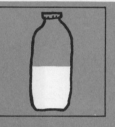

A half quart of milk is a fraction.

A quarter of a pound of butter is
a fraction.

And even the clock shows a fraction—
a quarter past twelve.

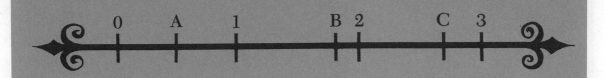

Fractions also can be parts of numbers. On this number line, the places marked A, B, and C are fractions because they are between whole numbers. In other words, the places marked A, B, and C are parts of whole numbers.

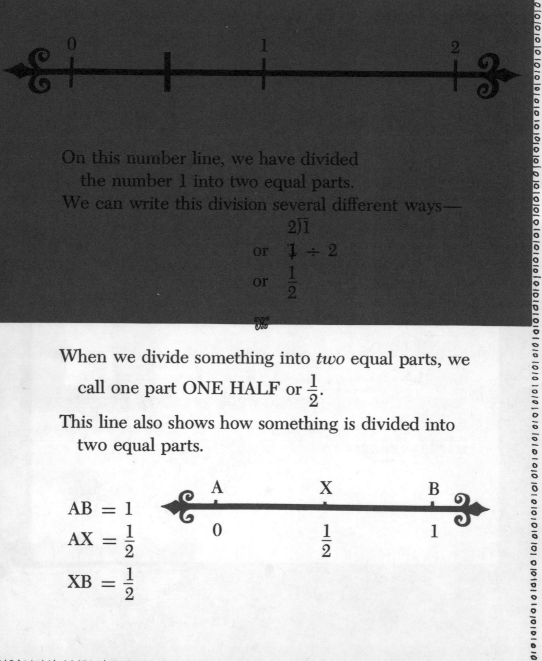

On this number line, we have divided
the number 1 into two equal parts.
We can write this division several different ways—

$$2\overline{)1}$$
$$\text{or} \quad 1 \div 2$$
$$\text{or} \quad \frac{1}{2}$$

When we divide something into *two* equal parts, we
call one part ONE HALF or $\frac{1}{2}$.

This line also shows how something is divided into
two equal parts.

AB $= 1$
AX $= \frac{1}{2}$
XB $= \frac{1}{2}$

This is ONE HALF or $\frac{1}{2}$ of an orange.

This is ONE HALF or $\frac{1}{2}$ of a glass of milk.

This is ONE HALF or $\frac{1}{2}$ of a pie.

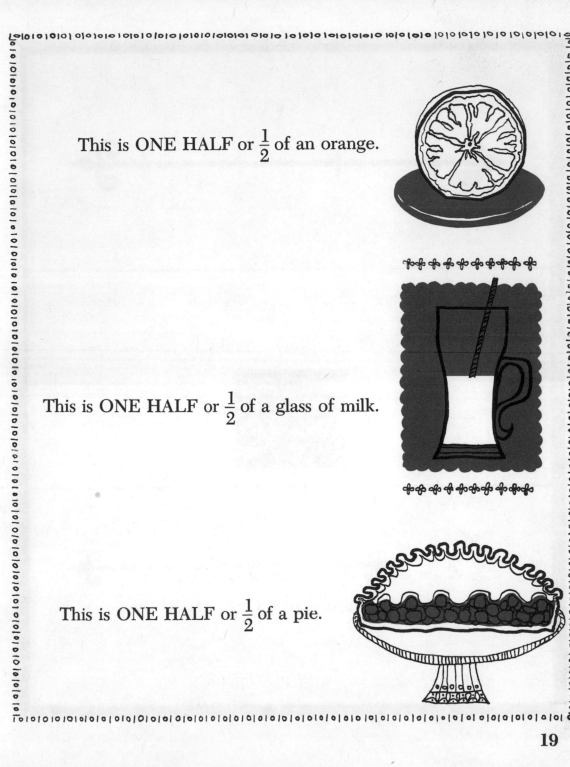

On this number line, we have divided the number
1 into three equal parts.
We can write this division several different ways—

$$3\overline{)1}$$
$$\text{or} \quad 1 \div 3$$
$$\text{or} \quad \frac{1}{3}$$

When we divide something into *three* equal
parts, we call one part ONE THIRD or $\frac{1}{3}$.

On this number line, we have divided the
number 1 into four equal parts.
We can write this division as—

$$4\overline{)1}$$
$$\text{or} \quad 1 \div 4$$
$$\text{or} \quad \frac{1}{4}$$

When we divide something into *four* equal parts,

we call one part ONE FOURTH or $\frac{1}{4}$.

When we divide something into *five* equal parts, we call one part ONE FIFTH or $\frac{1}{5}$.

When we divide something into *six* equal parts, we call one part ONE SIXTH or $\frac{1}{6}$.

When we divide something into *seven* equal parts, we call one part ONE SEVENTH or $\frac{1}{7}$.

When we divide something into *eight* equal parts, we call one part ONE EIGHTH or $\frac{1}{8}$.

When we divide something into *nine* equal parts, we call one part ONE NINTH or $\frac{1}{9}$.

When we divide something into ten equal parts, we call one part ONE TENTH or $\frac{1}{10}$.

When we divide something into *eleven* equal parts, what do you think one part is called?

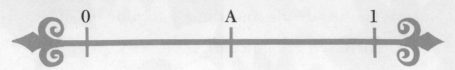

1. On this number line, what do we call the fraction that A stands for?

2. On this number line, what do we call the fraction that B stands for?

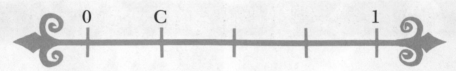

3. On this number line, what do we call the fraction that C stands for?

Correct Answers:

1. One half or $\frac{1}{2}$.

2. One third or $\frac{1}{3}$.

3. One fourth or $\frac{1}{4}$.

A fraction also can be part of a set.
$\frac{1}{2}$ of this set of 8 flowers is 4 flowers.

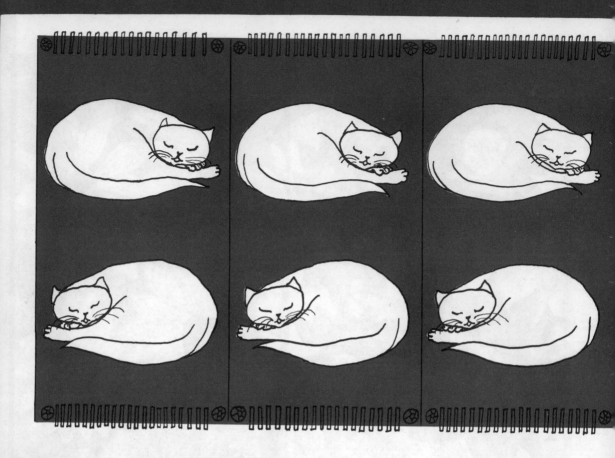

$\frac{1}{6}$ of this set of 12 cats is 2 cats.

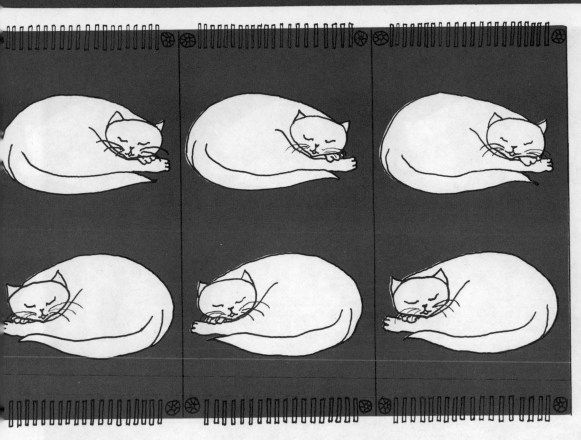

What is $\frac{1}{3}$ of this set? $\frac{1}{3}$ of this set of 12 cats is 4 cats.

Test Yourself

1. $\frac{1}{2}$ of this set of 12 dogs is how many?

2. $\frac{1}{3}$ of this set of 12 dogs is how many?

3. $\frac{1}{4}$ of this set of 12 dogs is how many?

4. $\frac{1}{6}$ of this set of 12 dogs is how many?

5. $\frac{1}{12}$ of this set of 12 dogs is how many?

Correct answers:

1. $\frac{1}{2}$ is 6 dogs.

2. $\frac{1}{3}$ is 4 dogs.

3. $\frac{1}{4}$ is 3 dogs.

4. $\frac{1}{6}$ is 2 dogs.

5. $\frac{1}{12}$ is 1 dog.

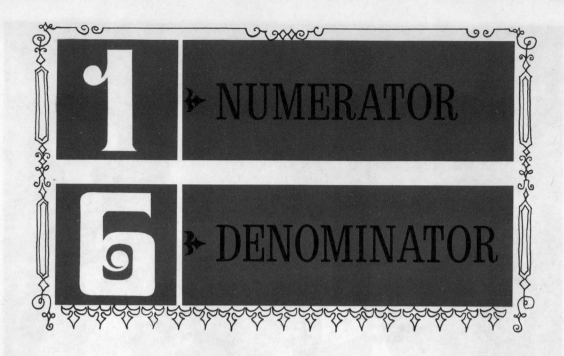

1 ← NUMERATOR

6 ← DENOMINATOR

You need to know the names of the two numbers in a fraction to understand how to use them.

The number on the bottom of a fraction is called the DENOMINATOR. The denominator names the parts. It tells how many equal parts something has been divided into. In the fraction above, the denominator is 6. This tells us that something has been divided into 6 equal parts.

The number on the top of a fraction is called the NUMERATOR. It tells how many of the equal parts the fraction has. In the fraction above, the numerator is 1. This tells us that the fraction has only 1 of the 6 equal parts.

In the fraction $\frac{2}{3}$ of a pie, the denominator tells

us that the pie has been cut into 3 equal pieces.
And the numerator tells us that this fraction
has 2 of the three pieces.

In the fraction $\frac{3}{5}$ of a cake, the denominator tells us

that the cake has been cut into 5 equal pieces. And
the numerator tells us that this fraction has 3 of the
five pieces.

In the fraction $\frac{3}{4}$ of a candy bar, the denominator tells

us that the candy bar has been divided into 4 equal
parts. And the numerator tells us that this
fraction has 3 of the 4 parts.

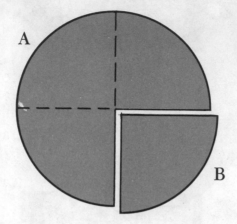

1. Part A is what fraction of this circle?

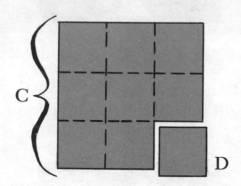

2. Part C is what fraction of this square?

Correct answers:

1. Part A is $\frac{3}{4}$ of the circle.

2. Part C is $\frac{8}{9}$ of the square.

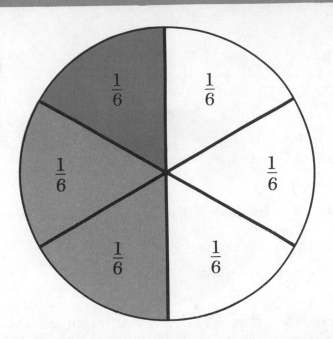

This circle is divided into 6 equal parts.

Each part is $\frac{1}{6}$.

The colored area is $\frac{1}{3}$.

All the shaded parts equal $\frac{1}{2}$.

You can see that $\frac{2}{6}$ is *equivalent* to (or the same as) $\frac{1}{3}$.

And $\frac{3}{6}$ is equivalent to $\frac{1}{2}$.

Equivalent fractions are pairs of fractions that
   represent the same number of sets or the same
   part of an object.

The sign = means equal, or equivalent.

This set of 9 hats has been divided into 3 equal parts.

We can say that one of the equal parts is $\frac{1}{3}$ of the hats. *Or* we can say one of the equal parts is $\frac{3}{9}$ of the hats.

So we can see that $\frac{1}{3}$ and $\frac{3}{9}$ are different names for the same fraction. $\frac{1}{3} = \frac{3}{9}$. They are equivalent.

We can say two of the equal parts are $\frac{2}{3}$ of the hats. Or we can say two of the equal parts are $\frac{6}{9}$ of the hats. They are equivalent.

So we can see that $\frac{2}{3}$ and $\frac{6}{9}$ are different names for the same fraction. $\frac{2}{3} = \frac{6}{9}$.

Here is a set of 25 sailors. It has been divided into 5 equal parts.

1. What are two names for the fraction A?
2. What are two names for the fraction B?

Correct answers:
1. $\frac{2}{5}$ or $\frac{10}{25}$

2. $\frac{3}{5}$ or $\frac{15}{25}$

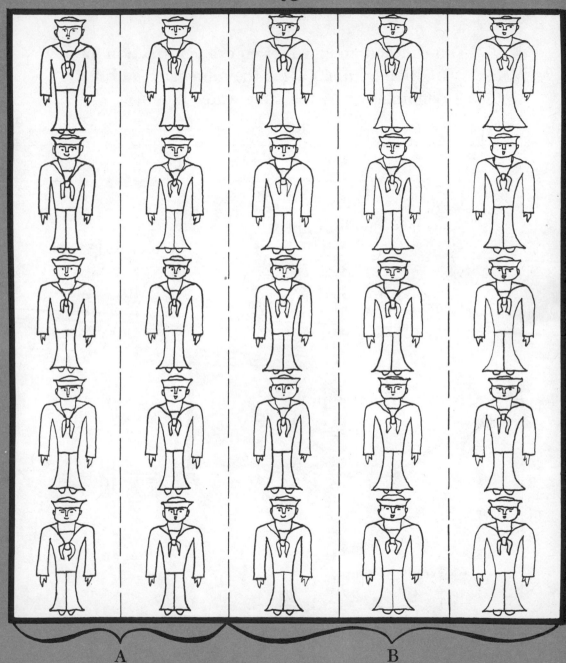

A   B

You can find an equal, or equivalent, fraction for any fraction by multiplying the numerator and the denominator by the same whole number.

❧

Here are some examples:

$$\frac{2}{3} = \frac{2 \times 7}{3 \times 7} = \frac{14}{21} \qquad \frac{3}{4} = \frac{3 \times 5}{4 \times 5} = \frac{15}{20}$$

$$\frac{3}{5} = \frac{3 \times 6}{5 \times 6} = \frac{18}{30} \qquad \frac{4}{9} = \frac{4 \times 10}{9 \times 10} = \frac{40}{90}$$

Now work these problems:

1. $\frac{1}{2} = \frac{1 \times 9}{2 \times 9} = \frac{?}{?}$ 2. $\frac{4}{5} = \frac{4 \times 7}{5 \times 7} = \frac{?}{?}$

3. $\frac{4}{6} = \frac{4 \times 5}{6 \times 5} = \frac{?}{?}$ 4. $\frac{3}{7} = \frac{3 \times 10}{7 \times 10} = \frac{?}{?}$

Correct answers:

1. $\frac{9}{18}$ 2. $\frac{28}{35}$ 3. $\frac{20}{30}$ 4. $\frac{30}{70}$

You know that division is the opposite of multiplication.
So you also can change a fraction into an
equal fraction by dividing the numerator and
the denominator by the same whole number.

ꙅ

Here are some examples:

$$\frac{7}{21} = \frac{7 \div 7}{21 \div 7} = \frac{1}{3} \qquad \frac{24}{30} = \frac{24 \div 6}{30 \div 6} = \frac{4}{5}$$

$$\frac{27}{72} = \frac{27 \div 9}{72 \div 9} = \frac{3}{8} \qquad \frac{28}{40} = \frac{28 \div 4}{40 \div 4} = \frac{7}{10}$$

Test Yourself

Now work these problems:

1. $\dfrac{19}{38} = \dfrac{19 \div 19}{38 \div 19} = \dfrac{?}{?}$ 2. $\dfrac{18}{27} = \dfrac{18 \div 9}{27 \div 9} = \dfrac{?}{?}$

3. $\dfrac{20}{28} = \dfrac{20 \div 4}{28 \div 4} = \dfrac{?}{?}$ 4. $\dfrac{40}{45} = \dfrac{40 \div 5}{45 \div 5} = \dfrac{?}{?}$

Correct answers:

1. $\dfrac{1}{2}$ 2. $\dfrac{2}{3}$ 3. $\dfrac{5}{7}$ 4. $\dfrac{8}{9}$

REDUCING

When you divide the numerator and the denominator
of a fraction by the same whole number,
it is called *reducing* the fraction.

To reduce the fraction $\frac{18}{36}$ you divide the numerator

and denominator by 18 and you get $\frac{1}{2}$.

❀

You usually want to reduce a fraction so that the
numerator and the denominator are the lowest
possible numbers, because smaller numbers are
easier to work with.

To reduce the numerator and the denominator to their
lowest possible numbers is called reducing the
fraction to its *lowest terms*.

It is not always easy to see what whole number should
be divided into the numerator and the denominator
to reduce a fraction to its lowest terms. So sometimes
you must do the division in steps, like this:

$$\begin{array}{ccccccc}
\textit{step 1} & & \textit{step 2} & & \textit{step 3} \\
\end{array}$$

$$\frac{56}{84} = \frac{56 \div 2}{84 \div 2} = \frac{28}{42} = \frac{28 \div 2}{42 \div 2} = \frac{14}{21} = \frac{14 \div 7}{21 \div 7} = \frac{2}{3}$$

$$\frac{56}{84} = \frac{2}{3}$$

Here are some rules to remember that will help you
  in reducing fractions—

If the numerator and the denominator both are *even*,
  divide each of them by 2. If they both still are
  even after you have divided by 2, then keep dividing
  each of them by 2 until at least one of them becomes
  an odd number.
If either the numerator and the denominator is *odd*,
  try dividing each of them by 3, 5, or 7.

Test Yourself

On a separate sheet of paper, try reducing these
  fractions to the lowest terms:

1. $\dfrac{50}{80}$ 2. $\dfrac{70}{140}$ 3. $\dfrac{64}{96}$ 4. $\dfrac{28}{112}$

5. $\dfrac{72}{168}$ 6. $\dfrac{36}{48}$ 7. $\dfrac{42}{70}$ 8. $\dfrac{48}{56}$

Correct answers:

1. $\dfrac{5}{8}$ 2. $\dfrac{1}{2}$ 3. $\dfrac{2}{3}$ 4. $\dfrac{1}{4}$

5. $\dfrac{3}{7}$ 6. $\dfrac{3}{4}$ 7. $\dfrac{3}{5}$ 8. $\dfrac{6}{7}$

CANCELLING

You can learn to reduce fractions more quickly
  if you learn to *cancel*. In cancelling,
  you just do the division in your head
  instead of writing it on paper.

Suppose you want to reduce the fraction $\frac{56}{84}$.

You see that both the numerator and the
  denominator are even, so you divide each
  of them by 2 *in your head*. Then you
  cancel the old numerator and denominator
  and write in the result of your division.
  It will look like this:

$$\begin{array}{c} 28 \\ \cancel{56} \\ \cancel{84} \\ 42 \end{array}$$

You see the numerator and denominator still
  are even, so you divide by 2 again. Then it
  looks like this:

$$\begin{array}{c} 14 \\ \cancel{28} \\ \cancel{56} \\ \cancel{84} \\ \cancel{42} \\ 21 \end{array}$$

Then you see that 7 can divide into both the numerator and the denominator, so the final steps look like this:

$$
\begin{array}{c}
2 \\
\cancel{14} \\
\cancel{28} \\
\dfrac{\cancel{56}}{\cancel{84}} = \dfrac{2}{3} \\
\cancel{42} \\
\cancel{21} \\
3
\end{array}
$$

Test Yourself

On a separate sheet of paper, reduce these
fractions to the lowest terms. Use
cancelling to make the work go faster.

1. $\dfrac{16}{128}$ 2. $\dfrac{20}{90}$ 3. $\dfrac{30}{42}$ 4. $\dfrac{20}{24}$

5. $\dfrac{72}{126}$ 6. $\dfrac{12}{36}$ 7. $\dfrac{28}{70}$ 8. $\dfrac{24}{64}$

Correct answers:

1. $\dfrac{1}{8}$ 2. $\dfrac{2}{9}$ 3. $\dfrac{5}{7}$ 4. $\dfrac{5}{6}$

5. $\dfrac{4}{7}$ 6. $\dfrac{1}{3}$ 7. $\dfrac{2}{5}$ 8. $\dfrac{3}{8}$

COMPARING FRACTIONS

You need to be able to tell which of two
fractions is the larger. In the signs in
the windows above, which store is offering

the best sale? Which is bigger: $\frac{1}{3}$ or $\frac{1}{4}$?

One way to tell the biggest fraction is to mark both
fractions off on a number line. This number line shows

us that $\frac{1}{3}$ is larger than $\frac{1}{4}$.

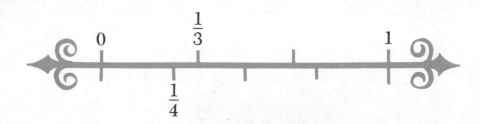

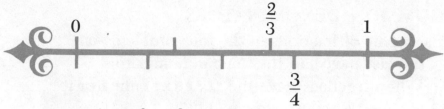

Which is larger, $\frac{2}{3}$ or $\frac{3}{4}$?

The number line above shows us that $\frac{3}{4}$

is larger than $\frac{2}{3}$.

But it would take a great deal of time to draw a
number line every time you wanted to compare
two fractions. There is an easier way.

Which is bigger: $\frac{1}{4}$ of a pie or $\frac{3}{4}$ of a pie? You

know that $\frac{3}{4}$ is bigger.

You knew the answer because
when the denominators of two fractions
are the same, you know that the one with the larger
numerator is the larger fraction.

Test Yourself

Which of these fractions is the larger?

1. $\frac{4}{7}$ or $\frac{1}{7}$ 2. $\frac{3}{18}$ or $\frac{12}{18}$ 3. $\frac{2}{5}$ or $\frac{4}{5}$ 4. $\frac{3}{10}$ or $\frac{9}{10}$

Correct answers:

1. $\frac{4}{7}$ 2. $\frac{12}{18}$ 3. $\frac{4}{5}$ 4. $\frac{9}{10}$

COMMON DENOMINATORS

Each pair of fractions in the four problems on
the last page had the same denominators.
When fractions have the same denominator it
is called a *common denominator.*

If two fractions do NOT have the same denominator
and you need to compare them, you must change
them so that they do have a common denominator.
This is easy to do. Just multiply the denominator and
numerator of one fraction by the denominator
of the other fraction.

Suppose, for example, you want to find out which

is larger, $\frac{4}{7}$ or $\frac{5}{8}$.

You do this:

$$\frac{4}{7} = \frac{4 \times 8}{7 \times 8} = \frac{32}{56}$$

$$\frac{5}{8} = \frac{5 \times 7}{8 \times 7} = \frac{35}{56}$$

Compare your answers.

It is easy to see that $\frac{5}{8}$ or $\frac{35}{56}$ is larger than $\frac{4}{7}$ or $\frac{32}{56}$.

Now, multiply the denominator and numerator
of the other fraction by the denominator
of the first.

Change the following pairs of fractions so that they
have common denominators, and then tell which is
larger.

1. $\frac{2}{3}$ or $\frac{5}{7}$ 2. $\frac{5}{6}$ or $\frac{3}{4}$ 3. $\frac{3}{5}$ or $\frac{2}{3}$ 4. $\frac{6}{7}$ or $\frac{5}{6}$

5. $\frac{2}{3}$ or $\frac{5}{8}$ 6. $\frac{7}{9}$ or $\frac{3}{4}$ 7. $\frac{7}{10}$ or $\frac{5}{6}$ 8. $\frac{7}{12}$ or $\frac{3}{5}$

Correct answers:

1. $\frac{5}{7}$ or $\frac{15}{21}$ is larger than $\frac{2}{3}$ or $\frac{14}{21}$.

2. $\frac{5}{6}$ or $\frac{20}{24}$ is larger than $\frac{3}{4}$ or $\frac{18}{24}$.

3. $\frac{2}{3}$ or $\frac{10}{15}$ is larger than $\frac{3}{5}$ or $\frac{9}{15}$.

4. $\frac{6}{7}$ or $\frac{36}{42}$ is larger than $\frac{5}{6}$ or $\frac{35}{42}$.

5. $\frac{2}{3}$ or $\frac{16}{24}$ is larger than $\frac{5}{8}$ or $\frac{15}{24}$.

6. $\frac{7}{9}$ or $\frac{28}{36}$ is larger than $\frac{3}{4}$ or $\frac{27}{36}$.

7. $\frac{5}{6}$ or $\frac{50}{60}$ is larger than $\frac{7}{10}$ or $\frac{42}{60}$.

8. $\frac{3}{5}$ or $\frac{36}{60}$ is larger than $\frac{7}{12}$ or $\frac{35}{60}$.

IMPROPER FRACTIONS

All the fractions we have used up to now
have had numerators that were smaller
than their denominators, such as $\frac{1}{3}$, $\frac{3}{4}$, or $\frac{5}{8}$.

These fractions are called *proper* fractions.
But when you begin to add, subtract, multiply,
and divide fractions, you will have to use
fractions whose numerators are larger than
their denominators. Such fractions are called
improper fractions. Here are two examples of
improper fractions:

$$\frac{5}{3} \quad \frac{7}{4}$$

To understand what these improper fractions
mean, let's look at the next number line.
You can see that $\frac{5}{3}$ is another way of saying
$1\frac{2}{3}$. And you can see that $\frac{7}{4}$ is another
way of saying $1\frac{3}{4}$. In other words,

*an improper fraction has in it one or more whole
numbers.*

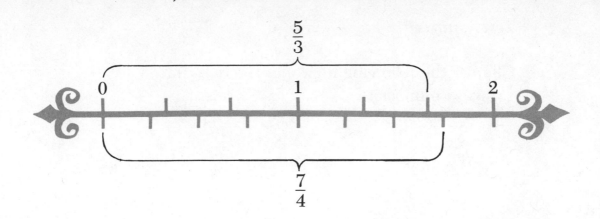

When you change an improper fraction into a
whole number and a proper fraction, this
new number is called a *mixed number*.

Two examples of mixed numbers are $1\frac{2}{3}$ and $4\frac{3}{5}$.

To change an improper fraction into a mixed
number, you divide its denominator into
its numerator.

For example, to change the improper fraction
$\frac{8}{5}$ into a mixed number, you divide 5 into 8

and you get the mixed number $1\frac{3}{8}$. To change

the improper fraction $\frac{43}{9}$ into a mixed number,

you divide 9 into 43 and you get the mixed

number $4\frac{7}{9}$.

Test Yourself

Change the following improper fractions into
  mixed numbers:

1. $\frac{23}{3}$ 2. $\frac{27}{4}$ 3. $\frac{43}{5}$ 4. $\frac{67}{6}$

5. $\frac{37}{7}$ 6. $\frac{59}{8}$ 7. $\frac{59}{9}$ 8. $\frac{67}{12}$

Correct answers:

1. $7\frac{2}{3}$ 2. $6\frac{3}{4}$ 3. $8\frac{3}{5}$ 4. $11\frac{1}{6}$

5. $5\frac{2}{7}$ 6. $7\frac{3}{8}$ 7. $6\frac{5}{9}$ 8. $5\frac{7}{12}$

You also need to know how to change mixed numbers
  back into improper fractions.

Let's change $6\frac{2}{7}$ into an improper fraction:

STEP 1

Multiply the denominator of
  the fraction by the $6 \times 7 = 42$
  whole number.

STEP 2

Add the numerator of the
  fraction to the result of $42 + 2 = 44$
  Step 1.

Place the result of Step 2
   above the denominator of
   the original fraction.

$$\frac{44}{7}$$

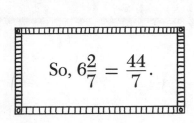

So, $6\frac{2}{7} = \frac{44}{7}$.

Test Yourself

Change the following mixed numbers into improper
   fractions. Use the three steps you learned above.

1. $5\frac{1}{3}$ 2. $4\frac{2}{5}$ 3. $3\frac{2}{7}$ 4. $9\frac{1}{2}$

5. $6\frac{3}{4}$ 6. $5\frac{5}{6}$ 7. $10\frac{5}{8}$ 8. $7\frac{3}{10}$

Correct answers:

1. $\frac{16}{3}$ 2. $\frac{22}{5}$ 3. $\frac{23}{7}$ 4. $\frac{19}{2}$

5. $\frac{27}{4}$ 6. $\frac{35}{6}$ 7. $\frac{85}{8}$ 8. $\frac{73}{10}$

ADDING FRACTIONS

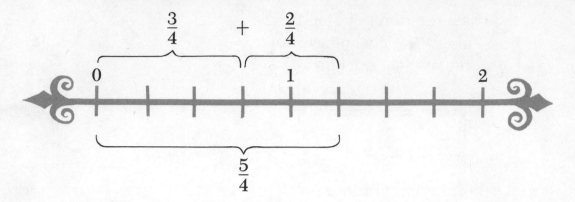

It is very easy to add fractions that have the same
   denominator. All you have to do is add the
   numerators and keep the same denominator.
The number line above shows:

$$\frac{3}{4} + \frac{2}{4} = \frac{5}{4} \text{ or } 1\frac{1}{4}$$

Here is another example:

$$\frac{5}{7} + \frac{3}{7} = \frac{8}{7} \text{ or } 1\frac{1}{7}$$

Test Yourself

Remember to add just the numerators and keep the
   same denominator in these problems:

1. $\frac{2}{9} + \frac{5}{9}$ 2. $\frac{3}{7} + \frac{2}{7}$ 3. $\frac{5}{9} + \frac{3}{9}$ 4. $\frac{3}{10} + \frac{6}{10}$

5. $\frac{2}{5} + \frac{9}{5}$ 6. $\frac{5}{12} + \frac{11}{12}$ 7. $\frac{7}{18} + \frac{8}{18}$ 8. $\frac{5}{6} + \frac{5}{6}$

Correct answers:

1. $\frac{7}{9}$ 2. $\frac{5}{7}$ 3. $\frac{8}{9}$ 4. $\frac{9}{10}$

5. $\frac{11}{5}$ or $2\frac{1}{5}$ 6. $\frac{16}{12}$ or $1\frac{1}{3}$

7. $\frac{15}{18}$ or $\frac{5}{6}$ 8. $\frac{10}{6}$ or $1\frac{2}{3}$

How do you add fractions that do NOT have the
same denominator? It's easy. Several pages
back you learned how to change fractions to
have a common denominator. So, when you have
to add fractions that don't have the same
denominator, all you have to do is change them
to a common denominator. And then you add them
just as you did the fractions on the last page.
Suppose you want to solve this problem:

$$\frac{5}{4} + \frac{2}{3} = ?$$

Step 1

Change the fractions to
    have a common denominator.

$$\frac{5 \times 3}{4 \times 3} + \frac{2 \times 4}{3 \times 4} =$$

$$\frac{15}{12} + \frac{8}{12}$$

Step 2

Add the numerators.

$$\frac{15}{12} + \frac{8}{12} = \frac{23}{12}$$

Step 3

Reduce the fraction and/or
   change it to a mixed number

$$\frac{23}{12} = 1\frac{11}{12}$$

Test Yourself

Use the three steps you learned on the
   last page to add these fractions:

1. $\frac{3}{5} + \frac{1}{6}$ 2. $\frac{4}{7} + \frac{5}{9}$ 3. $\frac{7}{8} + \frac{2}{3}$ 4. $\frac{5}{6} + \frac{8}{9}$

5. $\frac{14}{3} + \frac{3}{5}$ 6. $\frac{9}{4} + \frac{7}{10}$ 7. $\frac{11}{12} + \frac{2}{5}$ 8. $\frac{9}{7} + \frac{1}{2}$

Correct answers:

1. $\frac{23}{30}$ 2. $\frac{71}{63} = 1\frac{8}{63}$ 3. $\frac{37}{24} = 1\frac{13}{24}$ 4. $\frac{93}{54} = 1\frac{13}{18}$

5. $\frac{79}{15} = 5\frac{4}{15}$ 6. $\frac{118}{40} = 2\frac{19}{20}$ 7. $\frac{79}{60} = 1\frac{19}{60}$ 8. $\frac{25}{14} = 1\frac{11}{14}$

To add mixed numbers, follow these steps:

$$3\frac{2}{7} + 4\frac{1}{9} = ?$$

Step 1

Add just the *fraction* parts of the mixed numbers.

$$\frac{2}{7} + \frac{1}{9} = \frac{18}{63} + \frac{7}{63} = \frac{25}{63}$$

Step 2

Next, add just the whole numbers of the mixed numbers.

$$3 + 4 = 7$$

Step 3

Add the results of Step 1 and Step 2

$$7 + \frac{25}{63} = 7\frac{25}{63}$$

Test Yourself

Add these mixed numbers following the steps above.

1. $2\frac{1}{3} + 4\frac{2}{5}$ 2. $7\frac{4}{9} + 3\frac{1}{8}$ 3. $5\frac{3}{7} + 4\frac{1}{6}$

4. $12\frac{1}{5} + 7\frac{3}{8}$ 5. $9\frac{1}{10} + 6\frac{5}{9}$ 6. $17\frac{4}{7} + 5\frac{1}{4}$

Correct answers:

1. $6\frac{11}{15}$ 2. $10\frac{41}{72}$ 3. $9\frac{25}{42}$

4. $19\frac{23}{40}$ 5. $15\frac{59}{90}$ 6. $22\frac{23}{28}$

SUBTRACTING FRACTIONS

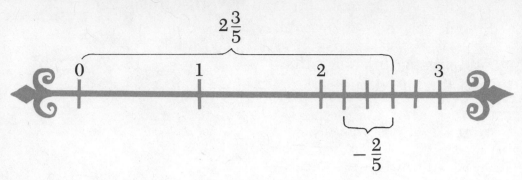

When you subtract a fraction from another number,
   you take it away from that number.
Suppose your problem is:

$$2\frac{3}{5}$$
$$-\frac{2}{5}$$

Look at the number line above. You can see that when

you take $\frac{2}{5}$ away from $2\frac{3}{5}$ you are left with $2\frac{1}{5}$.

So, when you are subtracting fractions that have the
   same denominator, you just subtract one numerator
   from the other numerator.
Here is another example:

$$5\frac{9}{10}$$
$$-\frac{6}{10}$$

Subtract the numerator of $\frac{6}{10}$ from the numerator of

$\frac{9}{10}$. You get $\frac{3}{10}$. Then bring down the 5. Your answer

is $5\frac{3}{10}$.

In subtracting fractions, if one fraction has a different denominator than the other, then you must change them so they have a common denominator—just as you do in adding. For example:

$$7\frac{5}{8} = 7\frac{5 \times 5}{8 \times 5} = 7\frac{25}{40}$$

$$-\frac{2}{5} = -\frac{2 \times 8}{5 \times 8} = -\frac{16}{40}$$

$$7\frac{9}{40}$$

Test Yourself

Work the following subtraction problems on a separate sheet of paper. Remember, if the fractions have different denominators, you must change them to a common denominator before you subtract.

1. $2\frac{7}{8}$ 2. $4\frac{10}{11}$ 3. $5\frac{8}{9}$ 4. $7\frac{4}{5}$

$-\frac{2}{8}$ $-\frac{6}{11}$ $-\frac{1}{9}$ $-\frac{3}{5}$

5. $5\frac{2}{3}$ 6. $8\frac{3}{4}$ 7. $3\frac{8}{9}$ 8. $7\frac{4}{5}$

$-\frac{1}{5}$ $-\frac{1}{3}$ $-\frac{1}{4}$ $-\frac{1}{2}$

Correct answers:

1. $2\frac{5}{8}$ 2. $4\frac{4}{11}$ 3. $5\frac{7}{9}$ 4. $7\frac{1}{5}$

5. $5\frac{7}{15}$ 6. $8\frac{5}{12}$ 7. $3\frac{23}{36}$ 8. $7\frac{3}{10}$

Before learning how to work harder subtraction
problems, there is one easy thing to learn
about changing a whole number 1 into a fraction.
Look at the cake above that is cut into three equal pieces.
Remember that the denominator of a fraction tells
how many equal pieces a number has been divided into,
and the numerator tells how many of those pieces are
in the particular number. Because all three pieces of the
cake are still there, $1 = \frac{3}{3}$.

In the cake that has been cut into four pieces,

$$1 = \frac{4}{4}.$$

And for the cake cut into five pieces,

$$1 = \frac{5}{5}.$$

In fact, you can change the whole number 1 into a fraction with *any* denominator and make the numerator that same number.

For example:

$$1 = \frac{14}{14} = \frac{78}{78} = \frac{193}{193} = \frac{2095}{2095}$$

If you have this problem, you can see that you cannot take $\frac{3}{5}$ away from $\frac{1}{5}$. To make the numerator of the fraction in the mixed number larger, you have to *borrow* a whole number 1 or $\frac{5}{5}$ from the 7.

Then you add it to the fraction part of the mixed number. You do it like this—

$$7\frac{1}{5} = 6 \ \frac{5}{5} + \frac{1}{5} = \ 6\frac{6}{5}$$
$$-\frac{3}{5} = \qquad\qquad -\frac{3}{5}$$
$$\qquad\qquad\qquad\qquad 6\frac{3}{5}$$

Test Yourself

On a separate piece of paper work these problems. In each one you must borrow.

1. $9\frac{1}{7}$ 2. $3\frac{2}{5}$ 3. $4\frac{2}{11}$ 4. $5\frac{1}{3}$
   $-\frac{3}{7}$ $-\frac{4}{5}$ $-\frac{7}{11}$ $-\frac{2}{3}$

Correct answers:

1. $8\frac{5}{7}$ 2. $2\frac{3}{5}$ 3. $3\frac{6}{11}$ 4. $4\frac{2}{3}$

MULTIPLYING
FRACTIONS

How much is $\frac{3}{5}$ of 20 owls?

If you look at the set of
owls, you can see that
you divide the set into
fifths and then multiply
by 3.

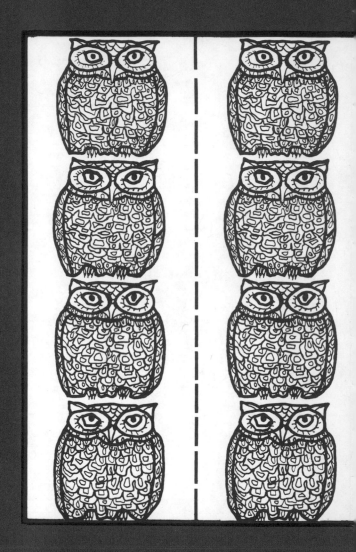

$$\frac{3}{5}$$

To work this problem with numbers, you do this:

Step 1

Multiply by the numerator

$$\frac{3}{5} \times \frac{20}{1} = \frac{3 \times 20}{5} = \frac{60}{5}$$

Step 2

Divide by the denominator

$$\frac{60}{5} = 12$$

$$\frac{3}{4} \times 83$$

To solve this problem:

Step 1

Multiply by the numerator.

$$\frac{3}{4} \times 83 = \frac{3 \times 83}{4} = \frac{249}{4}$$

Step 2

Divide by the denominator.

$$\begin{array}{r} 62 \\ 4)\overline{249} \\ \underline{24} \\ 9 \\ \underline{8} \\ 1 \end{array}$$

$$\frac{249}{4} = 62\frac{1}{4}$$

Test Yourself

Work these multiplication problems on a separate
sheet of paper. Remember that you multiply
with the numerator and you divide by the
denominator.

1. $\dfrac{2}{3} \times 18$ 2. $\dfrac{4}{5} \times 25$ 3. $\dfrac{4}{9} \times 27$ 4. $\dfrac{5}{7} \times 21$

5. $\dfrac{7}{8} \times 24$ 6. $\dfrac{4}{5} \times 19$ 7. $\dfrac{4}{7} \times 30$ 8. $\dfrac{5}{9} \times 25$

Correct answers:

1. 12   2. 20   3. 12   4. 15   5. 21   6. $15\dfrac{1}{5}$

7. $17\dfrac{1}{7}$ 8. $13\dfrac{8}{9}$

When you multiply one fraction by another,
you multiply their numerators together, and then
you multiply their denominators together.
You can make your work easier if you cancel
between the numerators and the denominators
before you multiply.

65

For example:

$$\frac{3}{8} \times \frac{2}{9}$$

Step 1

Cancel between one numerator
and one denominator

$$\overset{1}{\cancel{3}}_{8} \times \frac{2}{\underset{3}{\cancel{9}}}$$

Step 2

Cancel between the other
numerator and the other denominator

$$\frac{\overset{1}{\cancel{3}}}{\underset{4}{\cancel{8}}} \times \frac{\overset{1}{\cancel{2}}}{\underset{3}{\cancel{9}}}$$

Step 3

Multiply the numerators together
and then multiply the denominators
together.

$$\frac{1 \times 1}{4 \times 3} = \frac{1}{12}$$

So——

$$\frac{3}{8} \times \frac{2}{9} = \frac{1}{12}$$

Test Yourself

Work these problems on a separate sheet of
  paper and compare your answers with the
  correct answers below.

Some of the problems have mixed numbers—
  you will have to change these to improper
  fractions *before* you can multiply.

Some of the problems have improper fractions—
  you should make sure that your answer is
  reduced and changed to a mixed fraction,
  if necessary.

1. $\dfrac{2}{3} \times \dfrac{6}{7}$ 2. $\dfrac{4}{5} \times \dfrac{9}{16}$ 3. $\dfrac{17}{4} \times \dfrac{4}{5}$ 4. $\dfrac{34}{7} \times \dfrac{21}{22}$

5. $6\dfrac{3}{4} \times \dfrac{7}{8}$ 6. $3\dfrac{2}{3} \times \dfrac{13}{16}$ 7. $\dfrac{24}{5} \times \dfrac{15}{3}$ 8. $2\dfrac{1}{2} \times 3\dfrac{1}{8}$

Correct answers:

1. $\dfrac{4}{7}$ 2. $\dfrac{9}{20}$ 3. $3\dfrac{2}{5}$ 4. $4\dfrac{7}{11}$

5. $5\dfrac{29}{32}$ 6. $2\dfrac{47}{48}$ 7. 24   8. $7\dfrac{13}{16}$

DIVIDING BY FRACTIONS

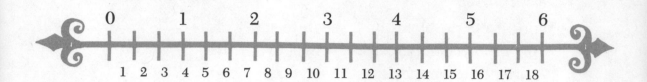

$$6 \div \frac{1}{3} = 18$$

You can see on the number line above that if you divide 6 by thirds you get 18 thirds.

And if you divide each of 6 pies by thirds, you can see there are 18 pieces.

So, when you divide by a fraction, you *turn the fraction over and then multiply*. Like this—

$$6 \div \frac{1}{3} = 6 \times \boxed{\frac{3}{1}} = \frac{18}{1} = 18$$

Study these other examples:

1. $8 \div \dfrac{3}{4} = 8 \times \boxed{\dfrac{4}{3}} = \dfrac{32}{3} = 10\dfrac{2}{3}$

2. $\dfrac{3}{4} \div \dfrac{2}{3} = \dfrac{3}{4} \times \boxed{\dfrac{3}{2}} = \dfrac{9}{8} = 1\dfrac{1}{8}$

3. $5\dfrac{2}{3} \div 7\dfrac{1}{5} = \dfrac{17}{3} \div \dfrac{36}{5} = \dfrac{17}{3} \times \boxed{\dfrac{5}{36}} = \dfrac{85}{108}$

Test Yourself

Work out these problems on a separate sheet
of paper. Then compare your answers to
those at the bottom of the page. In working
the problems, remember to turn over the
fraction that you are dividing by. Reduce
your answers, and if necessary change them
into mixed numbers.

1. $4 \div \dfrac{3}{4}$ 2. $\dfrac{6}{7} \div \dfrac{3}{5}$ 3. $8 \div \dfrac{2}{3}$ 4. $\dfrac{9}{10} \div \dfrac{3}{5}$

5. $6\dfrac{2}{5} \div 4\dfrac{5}{9}$ 6. $2\dfrac{2}{3} \div 1\dfrac{7}{8}$ 7. $3 \div \dfrac{6}{7}$ 8. $4\dfrac{3}{5} \div \dfrac{3}{7}$

Correct answers:

1. $5\dfrac{1}{3}$ 2. $1\dfrac{3}{7}$ 3. 12 4. $1\dfrac{1}{2}$

5. $1\dfrac{83}{205}$ 6. $1\dfrac{19}{45}$ 7. $3\dfrac{1}{2}$ 8. $10\dfrac{11}{15}$

WORD PROBLEMS IN FRACTIONS

Test Yourself

Here are some word problems in fractions.
   Think very carefully whether each problem
   calls for addition, subtraction, multiplication,
   division, or a combination of these. Check
   your answers with the correct answers on
   the next page.

1. Jean's mother bought an $18\frac{1}{2}$ pound turkey.

   Her cookbook says to roast it at 325° for

   $\frac{1}{4}$ of an hour for each pound. How long should

   she cook the turkey in the oven?

2. George did $\frac{1}{3}$ hour of homework on Math, $\frac{3}{4}$ hour on

   Social Studies, and $\frac{1}{3}$ hour on English. How many

   hours of homework did he do?

3. Bob bought $8\frac{1}{2}$ pounds of candy and divided it

   equally among his friends, giving each $\frac{1}{4}$

   of a pound. How many friends did he give candy to?

Correct answers to word problems on last page:

1. $18\frac{1}{2} \times \frac{1}{4} = \frac{37}{2} \times \frac{1}{4} = \frac{37}{8} = 4\frac{5}{8}$ hours

2. $\frac{1}{3} + \frac{3}{4} + \frac{1}{3} = \frac{1 \times 4}{3 \times 4} + \frac{3 \times 3}{4 \times 3} + \frac{1 \times 4}{3 \times 4} =$

   $\frac{4}{12} + \frac{9}{12} + \frac{4}{12} = \frac{17}{12} = 1\frac{5}{12}$ hours.

3. $8\frac{1}{2} \div \frac{1}{4} = \frac{17}{2} \div \frac{1}{4} = \frac{17}{\underset{1}{2}} \times \frac{\overset{2}{4}}{1} = 34$ friends

Now that you can add, subtract, multiply, and divide
fractions, you can see how easy it is to do
everyday problems with fractions.